Original title:
Breaking Free

Copyright © 2024 Swan Charm
All rights reserved.

Author: Liisi Lendorav
ISBN HARDBACK: 978-9916-89-988-5
ISBN PAPERBACK: 978-9916-89-989-2
ISBN EBOOK: 978-9916-89-990-8

Unveiling the Unchained

In shadows deep where dreams collide,
A heart awakens, cast aside.
Chains of silence break at last,
Echoes of freedom boldly cast.

With every breath, the past ignites,
A phoenix born from restless nights.
The spirit soars, no weight to hold,
Unchained stories quietly told.

The light pours in, a golden hue,
As hopes entwine, and fears undo.
In open skies, the journey starts,
A symphony of brave new hearts.

Unraveled threads of fate's design,
A tapestry where stars align.
The whispers soft, of love and fire,
Awakening a bold desire.

With every step, the world unveils,
A dance of dreams where courage prevails.
The unchained souls, forever bright,
In unity, they claim their light.

The Dance of the Unbound

In twilight's glow, the shadows sway,
A rhythm found in night and day.
Feet of freedom touch the ground,
In every heart, a pulse profound.

With swirling winds, the spirits twirl,
In open arms, we share the whirl.
Boundless laughter fills the air,
A joyful dance, beyond compare.

Each twinkle sparkles, vivid dreams,
Unfettered hopes that burst at seams.
With every leap, the fear rescinds,
Together we embrace the winds.

Eager hearts, like stars, align,
The night ignites a showcase divine.
In rhythms wild, we echo free,
The dance of souls, a jubilee.

Beneath the moon, our shadows play,
In sweet surrender, come what may.
For in this night, the world is ours,
A tapestry of dreams and stars.

The Pulse of Adventure

In the heart of the wild, I roam,
Chasing shadows of dreams untold.
Each step a beat, each breath a song,
I find courage as I unfold.

Through the mountains high, I climb,
With the wind as a companion near.
Every turn unveils new paths,
Whispers of freedom in my ear.

Under starlit skies, I wander,
The night cradles my wandering soul.
With every heartbeat, I discover,
Adventure's pulse makes me whole.

Threads of Self-Discovery

In the quiet moments of thought,
I weave together pieces of me.
Each thread a story, softly caught,
In the fabric of my identity.

Through the mirrors of time, I gaze,
Reflecting on choices made and lost.
Each lesson learned, a guiding blaze,
Illuminating paths, no matter the cost.

With each stitch of hope, I grow,
Unraveling fears that held me tight.
In the tapestry of self, I sow,
The colors of my heart burning bright.

The Liberation Tapestry

In chains of doubt, I felt confined,
But dreams like fire, they sparked my soul.
With courage as my guiding wind,
I broke the binds, I sought my whole.

Each voice of fear began to fade,
As strength emerged within my chest.
I danced upon the paths remade,
In my heart, I feel the zest.

The threads of hope entwine so bold,
Crafting a banner of my stride.
Each moment lived, a tale retold,
In liberation, I take pride.

The Canvas of Choice

Upon a blank canvas, I stand,
With colors vivid, dreams to express.
Each stroke a decision, a mark so grand,
Crafting my fate, I feel the press.

With brushes dipped in shades of fate,
I blend the hues of joy and pain.
In the gallery of life, I create,
A mosaic where loss meets gain.

What shall I paint in the light of day?
Each choice a whisper, a voice so free.
In this artwork of life, come what may,
I embrace the canvas that is me.

Through the Cracked Walls

Whispers travel through the cracks,
Secrets held by ancient stones.
Echoes of lives that once were,
Faint memories, a haunting tone.

Nature seeps through every space,
Vines embrace what time forgot.
Time-worn tales in shadows trace,
Silent stories, more than thought.

Footsteps linger on the floor,
Tracing paths of untold dreams.
Faded laughter, a distant roar,
Lost within the moonlit beams.

Hope still flickers in the air,
Nurtured by the light of dawn.
Strength dwells in the wear and tear,
New beginnings when night is gone.

Through the cracks, life finds a way,
Resilience blooms in every heart.
Walls may crumble, skies turn gray,
But from the dust, we will not part.

The Spirit's Serenade

In twilight's embrace, spirits dance,
Notes of freedom float on air.
Whispers of love and lost romance,
A melody beyond despair.

Softly strummed on strings of night,
Harmonies that break the chain.
Hearts entwined in fragile light,
An echo of eternal pain.

Through the woods, their voices glide,
Carried on the gentle breeze.
Rising with the moon's full tide,
Their song brings comfort, souls at ease.

In the stillness, shadows blend,
Every note a tale retold.
An invitation to transcend,
Crossing bridges made of gold.

As dawn awakens, silence reigns,
Yet the spirit's tune remains.
A gentle echo in our veins,
Unseen bonds that love sustains.

The Feathered Path

Soft and silent, wings take flight,
Guided by the stars above.
The feathered path shines in the night,
Leading hearts towards their love.

Each flutter tells a tale untold,
Of journeys both near and far.
In whispers, dreams begin to unfold,
A promise sealed in every spar.

Through fields of gold and skies of blue,
The feathers trail like hopes released.\nNature sings the songs so true,
A dance of peace that won't cease.

In every breeze, a spirit's call,
With every step, we find our way.
Together, we can rise or fall,
The feathered path is ours to lay.

So let us wander, hand in hand,
Through this endless, sacred art.
On feathered trails, we'll always stand,
With love and dreams within our heart.

The Fire of Resurgence

From ashes cold, a spark ignites,
Embers of hope begin to glow.
In the darkness, new life excites,
Awakening all we thought we know.

With each breath, the fire will grow,
Fuelled by passion, fierce and bright.
Through every struggle, we will show,
The strength that rises with the light.

Flames dance with untamed delight,
Casting shadows that shift and sway.
In this chaos, we find our sight,
Guided by the warmth of day.

Rekindled dreams take to the sky,
High above the doubts and fears.
In the blaze, our spirits fly,
A symphony that time endears.

Through trials faced, we learn to fight,
With fire forged, our spirits sing.
In resurgence, we find our might,
A testament to everything.

Voices of the Unstoppable

In shadows deep, they rise with might,
Their voices strong, breaking the night.
With every step, they shatter chains,
Unyielding hearts, where courage reigns.

Through whispered fears, they make their stand,
A force of hope, a guiding hand.
Together they march, they find their way,
With dreams ignited, they seize the day.

The echoes call, they cannot fall,
For in their strength, they stand for all.
In unity's bond, they claim their fate,
Voices of change, it's not too late.

Constellations of Courage

Stars above, a map of light,
Constellations shining bright.
Each brave heart a shining flame,
Together, they forge their name.

In the darkness, they find their way,
Guided by hope, they'll not delay.
Each story told, a beacon strong,
In the silence, they all belong.

Their journeys weave a tapestry,
Of courage vast, like the deep sea.
With every challenge, they rise anew,
Constellations bold, forever true.

The Escape Artist's Muse

In the shadows where dreams take flight,
The escape artist dances in night.
With nimble grace, they slip through time,
Finding freedom in rhythm and rhyme.

A canvas vast, an open door,
They sketch new worlds, embrace the lore.
Each leap an act of defiance bright,
Capturing stars, defying the night.

With every heartbeat, they craft their tale,
In a symphony bold, they cannot fail.
The muse of freedom whispers sweet,
In every struggle, they find their beat.

Beyond the Familiar Shore

Waves whisper softly, calling me near,
Beyond the shore, there's nothing to fear.
In the unknown, treasures await,
A journey grand, it's never too late.

With the wind at my back, I set my sail,
To chase the horizon, to follow the trail.
Each wave a promise, each tide a song,
In the arms of adventure, I truly belong.

The stars guide me through night's embrace,
In every challenge, I find my place.
Beyond the familiar, I dare to explore,
With heart wide open, I long for more.

The Thrill of New Beginnings

In the hush of morning light,
New hopes begin to soar.
Every heart beats a little bright,
Yearning to explore.

With each step comes a feeling,
A dance of brave and bold.
Wings of change are revealing,
Stories yet untold.

The shadows start retreating,
As courage takes its place.
Dreams and goals are competing,
In this newfound space.

Whispers in the wind call,
Promises hang in the air.
Rise up, surrender to it all,
Time to shed your care.

Festivals of laughter ring,
As joy begins to blend.
Life's a song we all can sing,
With each twist and bend.

Watercolor Dreams Unfurling

Brush strokes of the heart,
Spread across canvas wide.
In colors, dreams impart,
  A flow we cannot hide.

Each hue tells a story,
Of hopes both bright and bold.
Crafting whispers of glory,
  In swirls of blue and gold.

Let the edges bleed,
Into realms yet explored.
Where the spirit's freed,
  And creativity's adored.

Where thoughts flutter and glide,
Like birds in endless skies.
With each stroke we decide,
  To create, let them rise.

In moments painting slow,
The world begins to gleam.
With watercolor flow,
We chase our vivid dream.

Breaking Dawn of Possibility

At dawn the world awakes,
A canvas fresh and bare.
With each decision takes,
New paths dance in the air.

The sun begins to rise,
Painting skies in gold.
In the morning's guise,
Life's mysteries unfold.

Voices whisper softly,
Of chances yet to find.
With every breath, we craft,
The future in our mind.

Stepping through the haze,
Faith blooms with each new day.
In the light's embrace,
We chase the shadows away.

The dawn of dreams ignites,
With sparkles all around.
In the heart's delights,
Endless joy is found.

Seeds of Autonomy

In silent soil we nest,
Seeds of thoughts take root.
From struggles, we digest,
A journey to salute.

Nurturing the dreams,
With patience we afford.
Each hope within us gleams,
Awaiting to be poured.

We cultivate our voice,
With wisdom gathered close.
Empowered by the choice,
We rise, we bloom the most.

Through storms and gentle rains,
Our strength becomes our guide.
In freedom, love remains,
In every step, we glide.

Growing wild and free,
Our spirits unconfined.
In life's vast tapestry,
Autonomy we find.

Rising Rivers

In the dawn's soft light, they flow,
Water gleams like silver, aglow.
Whispers dance on gentle streams,
Nature's pulse, in vibrant dreams.

Mountains cradle their steady path,
Carving valleys, a soothing bath.
Echoes of the earth's own sigh,
Underneath the endless sky.

With each bend, a story told,
Of ancient journeys, brave and bold.
From the peaks to ocean's sway,
Rising rivers find their way.

Twilight drapes the shores in gold,
Dancing ripples, tales unfold.
Life awakens, swells with pride,
In this flow, we all abide.

As night descends, reflections gleam,
Stars are mirrored in the stream.
Rising rivers, endlessly,
Carrying time, wild and free.

Shadows Scattered

Beneath the trees where silence plays,
Shadows whisper soft, in grays.
Secrets linger in the air,
Mysteries twine with autumn's flair.

Flickering lights of fireflies roam,
Guiding wanderers safely home.
Every darkened path we trace,
Leads us deeper into space.

Clouds above, they drift and sway,
Casting shades that dance and play.
The world in tones of somber hue,
Whispers tales both old and new.

In the twilight, shadows blend,
Fading softly, they pretend.
Life's reflections on the ground,
In this quiet, solace found.

As night unfolds its velvet shroud,
Secrets veiled, the night feels loud.
Shadows scattered, wild and free,
In their depths, we seek to see.

Paths of the Unclaimed

Through forests deep where silence reigns,
Unclaimed paths weave through the plains.
Footsteps echo, faint and rare,
Nature whispers, unaware.

Twisting trails of grass and bramble,
Eyes wide open, hearts will ramble.
Seeking stories lost in time,
In the wild, we seek to climb.

Every turn a brand new chance,
To dance with fate, in wild expanse.
Where the wildflowers softly sway,
Paths unfold in bright array.

Time is fleeting, but here we stand,
Tracing lines in the soft sand.
Paths unclaimed, a promise bright,
Guiding dreams into the night.

So let the journey find its way,
In the uncharted, we will play.
With every step, our spirits soar,
Paths of the unclaimed, evermore.

The Threadbare Road

A winding path of shattered stone,
Holds the tales of those alone.
Each weary step, a story shared,
On this threadbare road, souls bared.

Once it sparkled, bright and new,
Now it whispers of journeys few.
Footprints linger, soft and faint,
Echoing the lost, the quaint.

Trees stand witness, tall and wise,
Underneath the open skies.
Guide the lost with gentle grace,
On this threadbare road, we trace.

Yet hope springs forth from every crack,
Resilience blooms where few look back.
In the shadows, light will flow,
On this road, we learn to grow.

Every heartbeat, every rhyme,
Threads the needle of our time.
Though worn, this road still leads us home,
On this threadbare road we roam.

Liberation's Whisper

In the hush of dawn's embrace,
Freedom stirs with gentle grace.
Chains that bind begin to break,
Awakening the heart to wake.

Voices rise like songs in air,
Echoes of a world laid bare.
Hope ignites the starlit night,
Guiding souls toward the light.

Through fields of doubt, we wander bold,
Stories of the brave retold.
Each step taken, trust unfolds,
Dreams like rivers, free and gold.

With every gust, the past will fade,
In unity, our fears are laid.
Together we will rise and soar,
Building bridges, opening doors.

Whispers soft, yet strong and clear,
Claim your path, cast off the fear.
Breathe in freedom, feel it flow,
In liberation's arms, we'll grow.

Beyond the Shadows

In the depth where silence dwells,
Whispers dance like secret spells.
Figures move in veils of night,
Fleeting dreams take timid flight.

Through the dark, a flicker glows,
A promise wrapped in fading throes.
Courage stirs, and hearts ignite,
Chasing phantoms into light.

Beyond the shadows, hope awaits,
Love transcends the heavy gates.
With each step, a strength will rise,
Beneath the vast and open skies.

In the twilight, dreams align,
Every breath, a sacred sign.
Together forged, we'll brave the storm,
In unity, we find our form.

So let the shadows fade away,
For dawn will break with vibrant sway.
With arms entwined and spirits free,
We'll shape the world, just you and me.

The Ties That Fray

Worn and frayed are bonds we hold,
Stories lived and tales retold.
Threads of love taunt and twist,
In the fabric, shadows persist.

Once so close, now worlds apart,
Echoes linger in the heart.
Faded moments weigh us down,
Yet in that weight, strength is found.

Fragile ties may bend and break,
But in their fraying, choices make.
Through the rips, light streams within,
New connections can begin.

With open hearts, we weave anew,
Crafting paths where dreams come true.
Though the ties may wane and stretch,
In their twilight, lessons etched.

So let the frayed threads guide our way,
Charting courses in disarray.
For even worn, they still convey,
The beauty in the ties that fray.

A Flight of Hope

From the nest, we dare to leap,
Chasing dreams that stir from sleep.
Wings unfurled in morning's hue,
A canvas vast, destiny's view.

Skyward bound, we rise and glide,
With every heartbeat, hearts abide.
Fear diminishes, courage calls,
In the winds, our spirit sprawls.

With every gust, we dance and sway,
Spirits high, we find our way.
Let the currents lift us high,
On the breath of dreams, we fly.

The horizon sings a siren's song,
Guiding us where we belong.
In this flight, we shed our fears,
Hope's sweet laughter through the years.

So take my hand and soar with me,
Together boundless, wild and free.
In skies of blue, we'll weave our fate,
A tapestry that won't abate.

Crossing Invisible Borders

Treading softly on hidden trails,
Where dreams and skies meet without veils,
Footsteps whisper through the dawn,
In silence, old barriers are withdrawn.

Hearts flutter with the taste of change,
In spaces where the wild feels strange,
Eyes wide open to the unknown,
In each heartbeat, a seed is sown.

Voices blend in the soft, sweet air,
With every breath, we cast away care,
Hands join in a dance of delight,
As we move beyond shadows of night.

Stars guide us through uncharted lands,
In unity, we make our stands,
Across the lines we forge new paths,
Embracing laughter, shedding wrath.

In the journey, we find our core,
With every step, we yield to explore,
Invisible borders fade from sight,
As we walk toward the endless light.

The Call of the Wild

In rustling leaves, a beckoning sound,
Nature's whispers, around us abound,
From mountains steeped in morning mist,
To rivers flowing where dreams persist.

With a heart of courage, we heed the call,
To dance with shadows, to rise, to fall,
The wild invites us with open arms,
In its embrace, we find our charms.

Through forest thick and golden fields,
Each step unveils what nature yields,
A world alive with electric breeze,
Where spirits soar and hearts find ease.

The thrill of adventure ignites the night,
In every moment, pure delight,
Animals play, and stars shine bright,
In harmony, we lose our fright.

So let us wander, let us roam,
In the wild, we craft our home,
Boundless, free, our souls take flight,
In the call of the wild, we find our light.

A Journey Beyond Limits

With open hearts, we set our gaze,
Wandering paths through life's maze,
Beyond the edge of comfort's shore,
In pursuit of dreams that we adore.

We'll cross the rivers, climb the hills,
Embracing challenges, feeding thrills,
Each turn reveals a brand new sight,
In the distance, our hopes ignite.

Clouds may gather, storms may rage,
But courage writes another page,
For every setback, a step we take,
In the journey, the past will break.

With every dawn, a promise made,
To chase horizons, never to fade,
For limits dissolve when spirits soar,
In these ventures, we learn to explore.

So here's to journeys, ours to chart,
With every breath, we play our part,
Beyond limits, we carve our way,
In the beautiful dance of yesterday.

Daring to Depart

With every heartbeat, a whisper stirs,
In dreams of journey, ambition blurs,
The call to leave our comforts behind,
To seek the treasures that life may find.

We gather courage, arms extended wide,
In the promise of adventure, we confide,
Every moment, a step we take,
Into the unknown, for our own sake.

Mountains rise and oceans spread,
From these boundaries, new paths are bred,
Across the distances, our spirits dance,
In the daring, we find our chance.

With laughter echoing through the air,
Our dreams take flight, free from despair,
As horizons shift, we dive and soar,
Forever seeking, forever more.

With hearts ablaze and eyes wide bright,
Daring the world to feel our light,
In the beauty of leaving, we unite,
Creating stories that burn so bright.

Seeds of Change

In the soil, dreams take root,
Whispers of the future sprout.
Hope is gentle as it grows,
In the quiet, the truth flows.

Every choice a tiny seed,
Nurtured by our thoughts and deeds.
Time will tell what blooms anew,
As the sun breaks through the dew.

Hand in hand, we plant and tend,
An open heart, the means to mend.
Through the struggles, we will rise,
With the courage in our eyes.

From the darkness comes the light,
Transforming shadows into bright.
Gathered strength will push us on,
Towards the promise of the dawn.

In unity, we forge the way,
Together, stronger, day by day.
With each step, our visions merge,
As we feel the strong surge.

Whispers of the Unseen

In the silence, secrets dwell,
Stories untold, a magic spell.
Echoes dance upon the breeze,
Carrying thoughts that aim to please.

Eyes are closed, yet we can sense,
Every shadow, every tense.
Voices linger in the air,
Gentle nudges, subtle care.

The unseen bonds that intertwine,
In a world that's so divine.
Trust the whispers in your heart,
For they guide us from the start.

Listen closely, can you hear?
Instincts call, they're always near.
Invisible threads softly pull,
Through the night, they're beautiful.

As we walk this hidden path,
Embrace the love, avoid the wrath.
In the quiet, life unfolds,
Carried forth by tales untold.

The Break of All Limits

In the confines of the mind,
Limits set, but still we climb.
With each heartbeat, courage swells,
Breaking free from all the spells.

Dreams are vast, like endless skies,
Fear dissolves as spirit flies.
Every barrier we erase,
In this bold, expansive space.

Unfurl the wings, embrace the air,
Leave behind the weight of care.
With every step, we redefine,
The boundaries that once confined.

Fuel the flame, ignite the fire,
Push beyond to reach desire.
Limitless, we find our way,
In the dawn of every day.

With each breath, we claim our fate,
Life is grand when we create.
Let the world see what can be,
When we dare to simply be.

Beyond the Boundaries

Past the walls that hold us tight,
Lies a realm of pure delight.
Discovering the unknown lands,
Where adventure always stands.

Ocean waves and mountain peaks,
In the vastness, freedom speaks.
Uncharted paths and starlit nights,
Guided by our inner lights.

Dare to venture, take the leap,
What awaits is ours to keep.
With each limit left behind,
New horizons we will find.

Together we will chase the sun,
In this journey, we are one.
Beyond the fences, wide and free,
Our spirits soar in unity.

Leave the doubt that dimmed your light,
Feel the magic, pure and bright.
In the boundless, we will thrive,
Living fully, so alive.

The Heart's Rebellion

A pulse that beats, against the chains,
Whispers that rise, breaking the reins.
With every thud, a silent cry,
For love unbound, to soar and fly.

In shadows deep, a fire ignites,
Dreams are conjured on starry nights.
Fists raised high, in defiant glee,
Take back the power, claim what's free.

No longer tamed by heavy sighs,
The heart refuses to compromise.
With every beat, a vow we make,
Stand tall and strong, for freedom's sake.

Through grief and pain, we find the way,
To trust the light, embrace the day.
A symphony of voices loud,
In unity, we stand unbowed.

With courage bold, our spirits swell,
This heart's rebellion starts to tell.
Together we forge the path ahead,
In love and strength, our spirit's wed.

Untamed by Design

In wild fields where grasses sway,
Dreams take flight, come what may.
The sun ignites each vibrant hue,
A canvas bright, waiting for you.

No walls confine this wandering soul,
Each step we take, we are made whole.
In rivers' flow, our spirits drift,
Exploring worlds, a precious gift.

With open hearts, we chase the dawn,
Where shadows fade, and fears are gone.
Through tangled woods, we'll carve our fate,
Untamed by design, we celebrate.

With laughter bright and voices free,
Embracing all that's meant to be.
In the chaos, we find our song,
In the wild, where we all belong.

So take my hand, we'll run and play,
Through dreams and hopes, we'll find our way.
Untamed, unbound, forever bold,
In stories shared, life's treasures unfold.

Uncaged Dreams

With wings unshackled, dreams take flight,
In starlit skies, they dance at night.
Each whisper soft, a gentle plea,
To rise above, to truly be.

When darkness falls, let courage rise,
In united hearts, the fire flies.
Through endless skies, we dare to soar,
Uncaged and wild, forevermore.

In vivid hues, the dawn will break,
With every step, new paths we make.
Paths unchosen, where hopes gleam bright,
Embrace the journey, embrace the light.

No longer trapped in grief and doubt,
Our spirits roar, we scream and shout.
In every heartbeat, our dreams align,
Together we shine, forever divine.

So spread your wings, feel freedom's grace,
In every moment, we find our place.
With open hearts, let laughter ring,
In the realm of dreams, our souls take wing.

The Loom of Liberation

Threads of courage, tightly spun,
In the loom of life, we are all one.
Each story woven, rich and bold,
Patterns of freedom, waiting to unfold.

In the fabric, a tapestry grand,
Of dreams and hopes, united we stand.
Each color bright, a tale to tell,
In liberation's embrace, we dwell.

The shuttle dances, side to side,
With every weave, our hearts collide.
Intricate designs, a shared vision,
In the loom of liberation, our decision.

No darkness binds, no chain remains,
In every fiber, the spirit gains.
With voices strong, in harmony's song,
Together we weave, where we belong.

So let the loom spin stories new,
Of freedom sought, of courage true.
In every thread, find strength and grace,
In the loom of liberation, we find our place.

Stitching New Beginnings

In the quiet dawn, we rise anew,
Threads of hope woven bright and true.
Every color sings a tale once lost,
Embracing the future, no matter the cost.

Stitching dreams with gentle hands,
Creating a life where joy expands.
Every knot a promise made,
In the fabric of now, the past will fade.

With every pattern, we find our way,
Guided by light in the light of day.
Fingers dance on fabric's grace,
A tapestry worn, a sacred space.

The fabric whispers, secrets untold,
Of love and warmth, and hearts so bold.
We sew together fragments of time,
Crafting a story that feels sublime.

Now we stand, our hearts in tune,
Beneath the bright and watchful moon.
Stitching new beginnings, hand in hand,
Together we weave, together we stand.

Voices of the Untethered

In the winds, the whispers fly,
Voices of the lost, they sigh.
Echoes dance in the open air,
Untethered souls, laying bare.

Through the valleys, through the night,
They sing of dreams taking flight.
Each note a story, wild and free,
A chorus of hope, a symphony.

From the shadows, they emerge bright,
Carving paths, redefining light.
Silent struggles turn to sound,
In unity, their strength is found.

With every heartbeat, a quest unfolds,
Tales of courage, moments bold.
The untethered rise, their spirits soar,
In the rhythm of life, forevermore.

Together they soar on wings of grace,
Finding solace in every space.
Voices of the untethered, loud and clear,
A testament that love holds dear.

The Unraveled Thread

Once tightly woven, now set free,
The thread unravels, a jubilee.
Loose ends whisper tales of old,
In every twist, a spark of gold.

What once was whole begins to fray,
New patterns form, come what may.
In each unravel, a lesson learns,
As the fabric shifts, the heart yearns.

Embrace the chaos, welcome the change,
Life's tapestry, beautifully strange.
Each knot a moment, binding and frayed,
In seeking the thread, new paths are laid.

The journey flows, the fabric bends,
What seems an end, a means to amend.
In every thread, a new vision grows,
Through unraveling, our true self shows.

In the dance of fibers, we find our voice,
The unraveled thread, our inner choice.
Each stitch a memory, woven with care,
In the art of living, love is our dare.

Where Hope Treads Lightly

In the garden where dreams take flight,
Hope treads softly, pure and bright.
With every bloom, a promise rings,
Wings of silver, gentle things.

Through shadows deep and valleys wide,
Hope finds pathways, a joyous guide.
It dances lightly on blades of grass,
In whispers sweet, the moments pass.

Starlit skies watch overhead,
As hope ignites the dreams we thread.
In every heart, a flicker stays,
A lantern glowing in the haze.

Where hope walks, sorrow takes a bow,
With every breath, we learn to vow.
Together we rise, through night and day,
In the embrace of hope, we find our way.

So let us wander where dreams renew,
In the light of hope, we find what's true.
Where hope treads lightly, love will grow,
In the garden of life, forever flow.

Unfolding Vistas

In valleys deep where shadows play,
The dawn breaks forth, a gentle ray.
Mountains rise, majestic and grand,
Whispers of time weave through the land.

Colors dance on the canvas wide,
Each hue a story, joy, or pride.
Beneath the sky, the rivers flow,
A tapestry of life on show.

Through golden fields where wildflowers bloom,
Nature sings, dispelling gloom.
With every step, new sights appear,
The essence of beauty, crystal clear.

Crimson sunsets kiss the night,
Stars awaken, sharing light.
In the quiet, dreams arise,
Unraveling truths beneath the skies.

As seasons shift, we learn and grow,
In every breeze, a gentle flow.
With open hearts, we journey far,
Finding solace in who we are.

Unscripted Realities

In the chaos, life unfolds,
Serendipity, a story told.
Moments fleeting, yet profound,
In every heartbeat, love is found.

Unplanned paths lead us away,
To hidden treasures where we play.
Laughter echoes through the air,
Life's unpredictability, we share.

With open arms, we face the day,
Embracing all, come what may.
In each mishap, a lesson learned,
For simplicity, our souls yearn.

Together we weave a vibrant thread,
In life's tapestry, joy widespread.
Moments cherished, memories bright,
Guiding us gently through the night.

So here's to life, unscripted and free,
Where every breath is a victory.
With hearts as guides, we'll surely find,
The beauty in the unconfined.

The Path of the Unchained

In shadows cast by doubt and fear,
The unchained spirit, bold and clear.
With every step, the chains fall down,
Embracing strength with freedom's crown.

Through fields of dreams and open skies,
The heart ignites, and courage flies.
Each obstacle becomes a friend,
On paths that twist but never end.

With scars of battles, stories told,
Resilience glimmers bright as gold.
In the wild unknown, we roam,
Finding solace, finding home.

The journey calls, a siren's song,
In unity, we will belong.
Together we rise, hand in hand,
Conquering fears, a mighty band.

So let us dance on life's great stage,
Unscripted, wild, beyond the cage.
With hearts unchained, we'll pave the way,
To brighter tomorrows, come what may.

Embracing the Horizon

Beneath the vast and endless sky,
Dreams take flight, learning to fly.
With every sunrise, hope is born,
A canvas waiting, unadorned.

In twilight's glow, we gather round,
Celebrating joys we have found.
Each whisper of wind sings a tune,
Carrying wishes, morning to noon.

As waves crash forth on sandy shore,
We discover beauty, wanting more.
In the distance, horizons gleam,
Inviting us to chase the dream.

With steady hearts and hands held tight,
We'll journey forth into the night.
Unfurling dreams beneath the stars,
Guided forever by our scars.

So here we stand, together bold,
Embracing horizons, stories told.
In unity, we find our way,
With love as compass every day.

Veils of Resistance

In shadows deep, we rise anew,
With whispers soft, and hearts so true.
We gather strength from silent screams,
Bound by hope, we weave our dreams.

Each step we take, a bold decree,
Defying chains, we seek to be.
In unity, we lift our voice,
Together, we will make our choice.

The veils that shroud will fall away,
As dawn unfolds, we greet the day.
With every tear, a tale is spun,
The battle fought, but never won.

We stand for all, against the tide,
With hearts ablaze, our truth the guide.
Each gesture fierce, a warrior's stance,
In defiance, we take our chance.

In mirrored lights, we see our path,
Through tempest's rage and quiet wrath.
Our souls ignited, spirits soar,
In veils of resistance, we want more.

Into Unrestricted Light

Unlock the doors that bind our fate,
Step into spaces, open, great.
With eyes wide set on distant skies,
We rise above, where freedom lies.

Emerge from shadow, stand up tall,
In unity, we shall not fall.
Our dreams like stars, they shine so bright,
Guiding our way into the light.

The world unfurls, its wonders bare,
Embrace the paths, let go of care.
We dance in sunbeams, warm and free,
To realms unknown, we're meant to be.

With every heartbeat, courage flows,
We reach for heights, where passion grows.
Into the wild, we break the night,
Together, step into the light.

Blossoms of Rebellion

From cracks in concrete, flowers bloom,
Defiant hues that chase the gloom.
With petals fierce, they pierce the air,
In gardens wild, we find our share.

Each blossom tells a tale of change,
In winds of hope, they rearrange.
With strength of roots, they push through strife,
In every bud, a spark of life.

Rebels rising with the dawn,
A tapestry of dreams reborn.
Their scents of freedom fill the breeze,
In whispered winds, we find our ease.

With colors bold, they stand their ground,
In every corner, beauty found.
Together we'll dance in the rain,
Through blossoms of rebellion, we gain.

Embracing the Unfettered

In open fields, we run and play,
With hearts unchained, we seek the day.
The wind it calls, a sweet refrain,
A promise made, we'll break the chain.

With every breath, we taste the air,
No longer bound by fear or care.
In laughter's echo, we are free,
Embracing life, just you and me.

Together we explore unknown,
In vast horizons, we have grown.
Through unmarked paths, we'll find our way,
With open arms, we greet the day.

Our spirits dance in boundless grace,
In every moment, we embrace.
With love as light, we'll always shine,
Embracing the unfettered, divine.

Unbound Horizons

Endless skies call to me,
With whispers of the sea.
Dreams dance upon the breeze,
In the light, my spirit's free.

Mountains rise, shadows fade,
In their majesty, I'm swayed.
Footsteps lead, paths untraced,
In nature's arms, I'm embraced.

Waves crash on golden shores,
Each heartbeat, the ocean roars.
Stars above, a canvas bright,
Guiding dreams through the night.

Fields of green, wild and wide,
Where my thoughts can freely glide.
With each breath, I find my way,
In this moment, I shall stay.

Hearts unite, love's refrain,
In the sun, we break the chain.
Together, nothing holds us down,
In this freedom, I wear the crown.

The Great Escape

Beneath the stars, a whispered plan,
To leave behind the mundane span.
With each breath, the thrill ignites,
As freedom beckons through the nights.

No more walls to bind our dreams,
In the silence, freedom screams.
With courage born from hope's embrace,
Adventure waits at every place.

Through forests dense, across the streams,
Life unfolds beyond our dreams.
With every step, a tale is spun,
In this journey, we are one.

The road ahead, a winding thread,
With laughter shared and fears unsaid.
We chase the sunset, hearts in flight,
The great escape into the night.

In our wake, the world will sigh,
As we dance beneath the sky.
Together, we'll forge a brand new path,
And live our lives, shed all the wrath.

Unfettered Soul

Windswept fields, I roam so free,
Nature's voice, a symphony.
Each moment wild, to live to learn,
With an unfettered soul, I yearn.

Clouds drift by, shapes in the air,
A canvas vast, I paint with flair.
With every color, life's a song,
In this space, where I belong.

Mountains high, valleys deep,
In their shadows, secrets keep.
With every breath, I feel the glow,
Of wisdom earned, the tides that flow.

Breaking chains, the heart's decree,
To find the self, to simply be.
In quiet moments, strength is found,
With an unfettered soul, unbound.

With laughter loud, or whispers soft,
We lift our dreams and soar aloft.
No limits set, the spirit flies,
A journey bold, beneath the skies.

Rise from Ashes

From the ruins, a flame ignites,
After storms, the sun invites.
In the silence, a new heart beats,
From the darkness, hope repeats.

Shadows fade, but lessons stay,
With each dawn, we find our way.
Resilience built to withstand the fall,
In this journey, we stand tall.

Cinders cool, but warmth remains,
Through our struggles, growth attains.
Fractured dreams can bloom anew,
In the light, we'll break on through.

Memories whisper, tales of old,
In their stories, courage bold.
With every scar, a new song penned,
From the ashes, we ascend.

Together we rise, hand in hand,
Building bridges, making plans.
In our hearts, a fire that glows,
From the ashes, a spirit grows.

Breathe the Boundless Air

In the morning light we rise,
With open hearts and clear blue skies.
The wind whispers secrets above,
Each breath we take is filled with love.

Mountains stand tall, touching the sun,
Paths uncharted, a world to run.
Mountains echo the songs of dreams,
In each heartbeat, a new world gleams.

Rivers flow with stories untold,
Against the current, brave and bold.
In every ripple, memories dance,
In the vast air, we take our chance.

Clouds drift softly, shadows play,
Guiding our steps along the way.
With every sigh, we share our souls,
Breathe deep the air, for it makes us whole.

Together we soar, far and wide,
Finding our truth, with hearts as guides.
In harmony, we sing our song,
In the boundless air, we all belong.

Through the Veil of Fear

In the depths where shadows lie,
Glimmers of hope begin to rise.
With trembling hearts, we walk the line,
Across the fog, our spirits shine.

Whispers echo in the dark,
Each faint voice ignites a spark.
Together we face the haunting night,
Through the veil, we seek the light.

Each step forward, a chance to heal,
Breaking chains that once were real.
In the silence, courage grows,
Emerging strength as fear bestows.

Illusions fade, the dawn appears,
The weight of doubt dissolves in tears.
Through the mist, we claim our grace,
Uniting hearts, we find our place.

So here we stand, invincible,
In the face of fears, we're formidable.
Through the veil, we now can see,
Bound not by chains, but by unity.

The Other Side of Bonds

In whispered threads, our stories weave,
A tapestry of hearts that believe.
Connections forged in the fire of trust,
In the dance of life, we must adjust.

With every word, a bridge is made,
Through laughter shared and fears displayed.
In the silence, bonds deepen strong,
A universal pulse where we belong.

The weight of pain is borne together,
As storms roll in, we face the weather.
Stronger together, we break the mold,
In the warmth of friendship, we turn to gold.

Time may test, but we won't break,
For love transcends each chance we take.
With open arms, we embrace the fight,
On the other side, we find our light.

So let us cherish this sacred tie,
In every moment, let spirits fly.
For bonds are not chains that bind our way,
They're wings that help us soar each day.

Revenant of the Wild

In the whispering woods, secrets call,
A spirit awakens, wild and tall.
Born of the earth, with untamed grace,
In the heart of nature, we find our place.

With every rustle, the echoes stir,
Through tangled roots, our souls confer.
The moonbeams dance upon the leaves,
In the wilderness, the heart believes.

The brook sings softly, tales of old,
A journey beneath the stars unfolds.
In the shadows where wild things tread,
We find the dreams that we once led.

To the mountains high and valleys low,
The revenant stirs, and we too glow.
In the rapture of dusk, we run free,
In the wild's grasp, we find our key.

So let us wander beneath the sky,
With spirits fierce, we learn to fly.
For in the wild, we're reborn anew,
In the dance of nature, we find what's true.

Veils of Sleep

In the silence of the night,
Dreams softly take their flight.
Whispers weave through shadows deep,
Embracing all who gently sleep.

Stars above twinkle bright,
Clad in veils of silver light.
Time slips softly, holding fast,
In a world where shadows cast.

Morning dew begins to rise,
Painting patterns in the skies.
Awakening the dreams we keep,
Lost yet safe in veils of sleep.

The moon bows low, a tender sigh,
As dawn breaks with a soft goodbye.
Shadows dance, then drift away,
Embraced by the warmth of day.

So cradle tight your dreams tonight,
In the tender folds of night.
Tomorrow waits just out of reach,
In the lessons night can teach.

Wheeling into Tomorrow

On the cusp of dawn's new light,
Wheeling forward, taking flight.
The horizon calls, a siren's song,
Where all the hearts and hopes belong.

Moments fleeting, ticking by,
Like the clouds that drift and sigh.
With each breath, a chance to soar,
Toward the dreams we can't ignore.

Fleeting shadows bid goodbye,
As the sun ascends the sky.
With a canvas fresh and wide,
We paint our paths, refuse to hide.

Hands reaching for the stars above,
Guided by the light of love.
Chasing echoes of the past,
Into tomorrow, shadows cast.

So spin the wheel, embrace the day,
Let worries drift and fade away.
For every chance the dawn will bring,
Is a new song for us to sing.

Hearts that Wander

Hearts that wander, roam so free,
Searching for a place to be.
In the twilight, dreams take flight,
Chasing whispers in the night.

Paths entwined like rivers flow,
Through the valleys high and low.
Each step taken, a story spun,
Beneath the glow of the setting sun.

Memories linger, fade away,
Like the colors of the day.
Yet in the heart, they softly glow,
Lighting paths where we cannot go.

Finding solace in the stars,
Wandering beneath their scars.
The universe, a friend so dear,
Guiding us through every fear.

So let us roam, let spirits soar,
Together, we will seek for more.
In every corner, near and far,
We trace our dreams, a guiding star.

The Garden Beyond the Gate

Beyond the gate, a garden lies,
Where every color meets the skies.
Petals dancing in gentle breeze,
Whispering secrets among the trees.

Sunlight filters through the leaves,
Casting shadows that softly weave.
A tapestry of life and cheer,
Inviting all who wander near.

Each bloom opens, a story told,
In shades of crimson, blue, and gold.
Butterflies, a fleeting grace,
Flutter in a joyous race.

A symphony of scents so sweet,
Where heart and nature gently meet.
In every nook, a peace unfolds,
As the magic of the garden molds.

So linger long, let time stand still,
In this haven, feel the thrill.
For the garden beyond the gate,
Holds the key to dreams inherent fate.

Wings Unfurled

In the quiet shade of dawn's embrace,
A whisper stirs in the tranquil space.
Softly the echoes of freedom call,
Inviting the hearts that yearn to sprawl.

Bright the horizon painted anew,
With dreams awoken and skies so blue.
A fluttered heartbeat beneath the skin,
Where hopes take flight and love begins.

Unfurl the wings, let the spirits rise,
Dance on the whispers of endless skies.
Together we soar, unbound and free,
Writing our tales in the symphony.

With every heartbeat, a promise made,
Through shadows deep, we won't be swayed.
Hand in hand, we face the light,
In the embrace of the coming night.

Wings unfurled, as one we'll glide,
In unity's warmth, we shall abide.
No chains can hold what the heart can feel,
In the vast expanse, our fates reveal.

Chains of Yesterday

Rusty links of a bygone time,
Echoes of laughter, a distant chime.
The weight of sorrow, a heavy tread,
Yet in the heart, hope's whispers spread.

From shadows cast by history's hand,
We rise anew, breaking the stand.
Each chain shattered, a story untold,
In the strength of the young and the old.

Lessons learned from battles fought,
In the fires of struggle, courage sought.
With every tear, a cleansing rain,
Washing away the remnants of pain.

Chains of yesterday, though hard to bear,
Forge the path we're meant to share.
Together we lift, together we stand,
Crafting a future, hand in hand.

The dawn breaks soft on the horizon line,
A reminder that even the stars must shine.
With every heartbeat, the past grows dim,
In the melody of life's sweet hymn.

Emancipation Dawn

A gentle light spills over the hills,
Awakening dreams, igniting souls.
Hands once bound now reach for the sky,
With every heartbeat, we learn to fly.

No more the shackles that held us tight,
Emancipation dawn, a glorious sight.
With courage ignited like a roaring flame,
Together we'll rise, we are not the same.

With every sunrise, new chances gleaned,
A vision of freedom, fierce and keen.
For in our spirits, the fire aligns,
Guiding our steps as structure unwinds.

Through valleys of loss, we tread with grace,
Transforming the shadows with love's embrace.
A radiant chorus, a symphony's sound,
In the heart of the dawn, we're truly found.

Emancipation, the anthem we sing,
A world reborn, with hope on the wing.
Our voices united, echo so clear,
Celebrating life, in joy, we hear.

The Shattered Cage

Beneath the weight of a fractured past,
A spirit stirs, no longer cast.
The bars that held are broken wide,
In the heart of a storm, we choose to bide.

Through shattered glass and echoes loud,
We rise to courage, resolute and proud.
No longer captive to fear or despair,
In the embrace of freedom, we share.

Each piece of glass, a lesson learned,
For every heart that bravely yearned.
With wings set free, we dance and play,
Turning the night into a bright day.

The shattered cage, now a distant tale,
Our spirits soar where dreams prevail.
United we stand in the light of the sun,
Embracing the journey that's just begun.

So rise with me, let's break this mold,
In the fire of hope, our stories unfold.
No more the cage, but the vast expanse,
In the freedom of life, we take our chance.

Dreams of the Unchained

In the depths of night, we drift and sigh,
Whispers of freedom twinkle like stars,
Boundless visions dance before closed eyes,
Yearning hearts break free from their bars.

With every pulse, new worlds emerge,
A tapestry woven in hopes and dreams,
We soar through fields where wildflowers surge,
Finding solace in moonlit beams.

Among the shadows, we release our fears,
Casting away the chains that bind our souls,
In the stillness, we cry untainted tears,
Embracing the magic as we become whole.

And in the dawn, when reality calls,
We carry the light of our night's embrace,
For in our hearts, the spirit never falls,
An unchained dreamer in boundless space.

So let us dance on the edges of fate,
Breathing in wonder, embracing the new,
For each dream ignites a flicker of grace,
A journey begun with a hopeful view.

Fleeing the Enclosure

Behind the walls, we hear the echo,
Of laughter lost in forgotten days,
The flickering candle gently aglow,
Calls us to break free from dusty ways.

With every heartbeat, the walls grow thin,
A whispered promise of life outside,
Through cracks and crevices, we begin,
To chase the wild winds and take our ride.

The rusted gates creak with the wind's breath,
A sweet release from confinement's hold,
As courage unfurls, the fear of death,
Transforms into strength, fierce and bold.

We run through fields of untamed delight,
Where wildflowers sway in the golden sun,
With every step, we reclaim our right,
And find in freedom, our hearts have won.

So let the horizons stretch far and wide,
Fleeing the shadows of what used to be,
The aches of the past we now set aside,
In open skies, our spirits soar free.

The Light Through Grated Windows

Through iron bars, hope flickers bright,
A glimmer woven with morning dew,
Chasing the darkness, embracing the light,
Whispers of freedom in every hue.

Sunbeams dance on the cold stone floor,
Singing sweet lullabies of the dawn,
With every ray, we dream and explore,
The shadows of yesterday slowly withdrawn.

In the stillness, our souls start to rise,
Painting the walls with colors untold,
A mural of passion that never dies,
Stories of courage in shades of gold.

Each slant of light tells a tale of grace,
Breaking the silence, igniting the flame,
Defying the darkness with bold, tender trace,
We find our voices in freedom's name.

So let us bask in this radiant beam,
For life through grates can still be divine,
In every moment, we'll nurture the dream,
And find our path in the light that we shine.

Flocking Toward the Sky

When dusk settles softly on the land,
The sky beckons with hues of deep blue,
We gather in flocks, united we stand,
With wings open wide, ready to pursue.

In the chorus of life, we sing our song,
A melody woven in threads of the free,
Together we rise, where we all belong,
Chasing the horizons, just you and me.

With each flutter, we leave behind sorrow,
Pursuing a dream written high above,
We dance on the winds, fearless tomorrow,
A tapestry stitched with hope and love.

Stars in our eyes, we glide through the night,
With whispers of freedom that echo and bind,
Through currents unknown, we follow the light,
And leave our cares in the dusk behind.

So let the winds carry our wishes so high,
As we paint the canvas of endless flight,
Flocking together, we soar toward the sky,
Unified hearts igniting the night.

Beyond the Cage

Wings unfold in the quiet night,
Silent dreams take their flight.
Bars of steel fade from view,
A spirit, fierce and true.

Through shadows, hope will gleam,
Breaking free from a faded dream.
Underneath the starlit sky,
A heart prepared to fly.

Every whisper of the breeze,
Carries tales of new decrees.
Beyond the cage, a world awaits,
With open arms and golden gates.

Rising high on currents bold,
Stories of the brave are told.
Beyond the darkness, light will swell,
In freedom's arms, we find our spell.

No longer lost in the haze,
We emerge from our tattered maze.
Beyond the cage, our voices ring,
In unison, our souls take wing.

Rise of the Undaunted

In the face of fear we stand,
Hearts united, hand in hand.
Marching forth with steadfast grace,
The dawn reveals our rightful place.

Through storms that threaten to confound,
We rise, undaunted, valiant sound.
The echoes of our courage strong,
In darkest times, we still belong.

With every challenge that we see,
Together, we shall face the plea.
Against the odds, we make our claim,
A blaze of hope in wildest flame.

A tapestry of dreams we weave,
In unity, we choose to believe.
When shadows loom and fears ignite,
We forge ahead, guided by light.

A spirit fierce, a heart aglow,
In every struggle, our strength will grow.
Rise up, undaunted, lift your voice,
In every battle, we will rejoice.

Chains Cast Aside

Once bound by fears and silent cries,
We shed the past, let hope arise.
Chains that held us, cold and tight,
Now drop away, lost to the night.

With every step, we break the mold,
Our stories fierce, our spirits bold.
Through the darkness, we'll reclaim,
The fire that ignites our flame.

Voices rise in harmony,
Breaking free, we'll sail the sea.
A journey marked by scars and grace,
In every heartbeat, we find our place.

No longer shackled by despair,
With every breath, we breathe fresh air.
Together strong, we forge our ties,
In unity, our spirit flies.

Chains cast aside, a new dawn breaks,
In every heartbeat, true freedom wakes.
With courage fierce, we chase the tide,
Together in this brave new ride.

The Horizon Awaits

Gaze upon the distant shore,
Where dreams ignite forevermore.
The horizon calls with open arms,
A world of wonder, endless charms.

Every wave that kisses sand,
Whispers hope across the land.
With courage swelling, we embark,
To find our place beyond the dark.

In the colors of the setting sun,
A promise made, a race begun.
The stars will guide our way by night,
Leading us toward the light.

With every step, we seek the new,
The horizon waits for me and you.
In every heartbeat, dreams ignite,
Together, we will chase the light.

The journey ahead may twist and sway,
But with each dawn, we'll find our way.
The horizon awaits, so clear,
With open hearts, we disappear.

Chasing the Infinite

In dreams we wander, skies unbound,
Each star a whisper, waiting to be found.
We stretch our arms to grasp the light,
Chasing shadows through the night.

With every heartbeat, a story we weave,
In this vast cosmos, we dare to believe.
A journey endless, forever to roam,
In the dance of galaxies, we find our home.

Through trials faced, and fears laid bare,
We chase the infinite, hearts full of care.
With every step, the horizon calls,
An echo of wonder, through the vast halls.

In the silence of space, our hopes ignite,
An ember of courage, glowing bright.
Together we rise, hand in hand,
Chasing the infinite, across the land.

So let us journey, unafraid to roam,
In this adventure, we find our home.
With dreams as our guide and stars as our map,
We chase the infinite, bridging every gap.

The Tapestry of Tomorrow

Threads of dawn weave through the skies,
Painting hope where our future lies.
Each moment a stitch, a tale to tell,
In the tapestry of tomorrow, we dwell.

Colors of dreams blend, bright and bold,
Memories glisten like threads of gold.
Woven in laughter, stitched with tears,
A masterpiece formed through the years.

With every heartbeat, a pattern unfolds,
Tales of adventure, bravery retold.
Through shadows and light, we gather our might,
In the fabric of life, we shine so bright.

Together we stand, hands intertwined,
Creating a future, lovingly designed.
The loom of existence, ever expanding,
In the tapestry of tomorrow, forever landing.

So we gather our dreams, and share our fate,
In the tapestry of tomorrow, we celebrate.
Each thread a promise, each knot a bond,
We stitch a future, of which we're fond.

The Senescent Sky

Beneath the arches of an ancient hue,
The senescent sky whispers tales anew.
With clouds as pages, time gently flows,
In the twilight's embrace, soft twilight glows.

The sun dips low, a golden sigh,
Casting shadows where memories lie.
As daylight fades, the stars ignite,
In the heart of darkness, there blooms a light.

Amidst the silence, wisdom resides,
The senescent sky, where time abides.
Each constellation, a story of old,
In the fabric of night, our dreams unfold.

With every breath, we sense the change,
In the senescent sky, nothing feels strange.
We find our solace in cosmic flight,
Embracing the moments, both day and night.

So we look above, in wonder and grace,
Finding our past in the night's embrace.
The senescent sky, a canvas divine,
A reflection of life, eternally entwined.

The Thrill of Ascent

Upward we climb, hearts filled with fire,
Chasing the mountain, climbing ever higher.
With every foothold, a dream held tight,
The thrill of ascent, a glorious flight.

Through rugged paths and skies so wide,
We embrace the challenge, no fear to hide.
With winds that whisper, we forge ahead,
The summit awaits, where dreams are fed.

In the echo of peaks, our spirits soar,
With every challenge, we crave more.
A dance with gravity, we twirl and spin,
In the thrill of ascent, our journey begins.

Each step a testament, a story we weave,
In the heart of the mountain, we learn to believe.
As the clouds part ways, we reach for the blue,
The thrill of ascent, forever anew.

Together we rise, with courage as our guide,
Embracing the journey, with hearts open wide.
In the thrill of ascent, we find our place,
Climbing together, wrapped in grace.

Walls that Crumble

Beneath the weight of time's embrace,
Old stones begin to fade and break,
Each crack a whisper of the past,
Each fall a chance for new awake.

The ivy climbs with tender grace,
It wraps around the weary sighs,
With every twist, a dream rekindled,
In shadows cast, a hope still lies.

From dust to dust, we rise once more,
The echoes of our hearts remain,
In every breath, the strength we forge,
Through walls that crumble, love will gain.

As moonlight dances on the stones,
A soft reminder, bright and clear,
Though walls may tremble, hearts will sing,
For freedom's song is always near.

So let the ruins tell their tale,
Of battles fought and dreams reborn,
In every crevice, light will sail,
And guide us through the early dawn.

The Echoing Heart

In quiet chambers, whispers flow,
A heartbeat lost in time's embrace,
It thunders softly, shadows grow,
Each pulse a thread, each breath a place.

The memories drift like autumn leaves,
They swirl in currents, gently pressed,
With every echo, hope achieves,
A melody that will not rest.

Among the silence, courage grows,
Each thump a promise, bright and bold,
Beneath the weight of all that's chose,
The echoing heart refuses to fold.

So close your eyes, and feel it beat,
The rhythm weaves through night and day,
In every longing, love's retreat,
A symphony we find our way.

Together these echoes intertwine,
As stars align, they light the dark,
The echoing heart is yours and mine,
A stronger bond, a living spark.

Footsteps into Freedom

With every step upon the ground,
We shed the chains that held us tight,
The path ahead, a freeing sound,
Leading us into the light.

The wind it whispers tales untold,
Of places we've yet to explore,
With hopeful hearts and spirits bold,
We venture forth, forever more.

Across the fields, where dreams are sown,
Each footprint marks a brand-new start,
In unity, we find our own,
For freedom stirs within the heart.

An open road, a boundless sky,
With courage woven in each stride,
We journey on, we learn to fly,
Together, standing side by side.

The world awaits with arms spread wide,
Embracing all that we may find,
Through footsteps taken, we collide,
In harmony, as souls entwined.

When the Chains Melt

When chains of sorrow start to bend,
And hearts entwined refuse to break,
A fire ignites, our spirits mend,
In unity, we'll pave the way.

The burdens lift, like morning mist,
Releasing dreams once locked away,
With every heartbeat, love persists,
And leads us forth into the day.

The walls of doubt begin to crack,
With every word, the truth we tell,
Together rising, never slack,
For hope will bloom where chains once fell.

Through trials faced and battles won,
When darkness fades, and light appears,
In every moment, love's begun,
A tapestry woven from our tears.

So let us be the sparks that fly,
Transforming pain to strength anew,
When chains melt down, we touch the sky,
With open hearts, we'll break on through.

The Rebirth of Spirit

From ashes gray, a spark ignites,
A whisper soft in quiet nights.
The heart, once heavy, now takes flight,
Embracing dawn, breaking the night.

In shadows deep, the light shall rise,
Transforming pain into the prize.
With open arms, we greet the change,
A world reborn, no longer strange.

Each step we take, a chance to grow,
Releasing doubts, we're free to flow.
The spirit's song begins to play,
Melodies bright, chase clouds away.

Through storms that rage and tides that swell,
We find our strength, we find our spell.
The journey long, yet hope endures,
In every heart, the truth ensures.

Awake with love, we now reclaim,
The joy that echoes, not the shame.
With open hearts, let new life start,
In unity, we heal the heart.

Ascending Beyond Limitations

The mountain high, we aim to scale,
With courage strong, we shall not fail.
Each step we take, we rise with grace,
Boundless dreams in this sacred space.

The chains that bind begin to break,
New paths arise with each heartache.
In every doubt, a lesson learned,
A fire within, forever burned.

The sky above, a canvas wide,
With colors bright, in love we bide.
Beyond the limits, we shall soar,
With wings of hope, we'll seek for more.

Resistance fades, the spirit flies,
In unity, we'll touch the skies.
With every breath, we shatter walls,
In whispers soft, the freedom calls.

Together now, our voices rise,
With strength combined, we claim the skies.
A journey vast, forever bold,
Ascending high, our dreams unfold.

The Path to Liberation

In silence deep, the truth unfolds,
A journey brave, the heart consoled.
With each step taken, fears dissolve,
In light we trust, ourselves evolve.

The chains we wore begin to fade,
With every choice, new paths are laid.
The courage found in souls ablaze,
We walk our truth, in endless praise.

The pain once felt, a distant hue,
As we emerge, reborn anew.
With open hearts, we find our song,
A melody that sings along.

Through winding roads and trials fierce,
A trail of love, we now disperse.
With gentle hands and mindful grace,
We carve our truth, a sacred space.

Together bound, in unity,
We stand for all, for you and me.
The path to liberation shines,
With every step, our spirit aligns.

Journey of the Unchained

Once bound by fears, now free to roam,
In fields of gold, we find our home.
With every heartbeat, we reclaim,
The dreams we sought, no more the same.

The winds of change, they call our name,
A journey bold, we'll stake our claim.
With wings outstretched, we greet the sun,
The past behind, the future's won.

Through valleys deep and mountains tall,
We rise together, we will not fall.
In every struggle, strength reveals,
The power found in how love heals.

No chains can hold this spirit bright,
Together we embrace the light.
With every step, a promise made,
In unity, our fears allayed.

The journey vast, where love is gained,
A tapestry of hearts unchained.
With open arms, we greet the day,
In freedom's grace, we find our way.

Emancipation's Song

In whispers of the night, we rise,
Chains forgotten, dreams unbound.
With every breath, we break the ties,
A future bright and freedom found.

Voices lift, a chorus strong,
Braving storms, we march ahead.
United in this sacred throng,
On wings of hope, no heart will dread.

Fields once bare begin to bloom,
With seeds of courage, love will thrive.
In every heart, we banish gloom,
Together, we will dream alive.

From shadows past, our spirits soar,
With every step, a brand-new day.
Emancipation, we restore,
In unity, we find our way.

For freedom's song will never cease,
It resonates through time and space.
In our hearts, we find our peace,
Together, we shall leave a trace.

A Symphony of Defiance

Echoes of rebellion call,
With every beat, we stand as one.
In shadows deep, we will not fall,
A fire lit, our rights hard-won.

The drums of hope begin to sound,
A melody of strength and pride.
Through every struggle, we are bound,
In harmony, we will not hide.

Raise your voice, let courage ring,
Injustice trembles, truth will reign.
With every note, the proud will sing,
A symphony that breaks the chain.

In unity, we take our stand,
A tapestry of dreams and fights.
Together, we will shape the land,
And claim the day, ignite the night.

For when we join, the world will see,
A force unyielding, fierce, and bright.
In every heart, our love runs free,
A symphony that claims the light.

Flight from the Familiar

Beneath the stars, we seek our fate,
With restless hearts, we long for more.
The world awaits, a wide-open gate,
Adventure calls from distant shore.

In shadows cast by structures old,
We shed the weight of past designs.
With dreams as wings, our spirits bold,
We chase the sun, where freedom shines.

Nature's whispers guide our stride,
Through valleys deep and mountains tall.
With every step, we cast aside,
The chains of fear that made us small.

On winds of change, our hopes will soar,
To lands unknown, through skies of blue.
With open hearts, we dare explore,
The journey's ours, the path is new.

So take a breath, embrace the flight,
The familiar fades in newfound grace.
For life begins at each new height,
In every leap, we find our place.

The Pulse of Freedom

Deep within, a heartbeat strong,
A rhythm shared by one and all.
In every right a resounding song,
That echoes through both great and small.

The pulse of freedom, bold and true,
With every beat, we stand as one.
In shades of red, in skies of blue,
A legacy that can't be undone.

From fields of struggle, roots run deep,
Nurtured by the pain and strife.
With courage sown, we dream and leap,
A tapestry of hopeful life.

In every heart, the fire burns bright,
With threads of justice, beauty weaves.
Together, we will claim the night,
And rise again, for free we believe.

For freedom's pulse will never fade,
It beats in time with all our souls.
In unity, our hope parade,
Together, we embrace our goals.

Wings of Liberation

In the quiet of night, dreams take flight,
Moments of silence, bathed in light.
Releasing the tether, the heart finds its way,
To soar through the skies, in freedom's sway.

Chains of the past, broken and tossed,
Each tear transformed, no more embossed.
With every heartbeat, a new song is sung,
The dance of the fearless, forever young.

Mountains of doubt, crumble to dust,
With hope as the armor, we learn to trust.
Through valleys of despair, we rise and we climb,
In the wings of liberation, we're free of time.

Let the winds carry whispers, soft and clear,
A melody of courage, for all who can hear.
Through storms we are guided, together we stand,
In the freedom we cherish, hand in hand.

Joyful we travel, on paths unknown,
Embracing the journey, never alone.
In the wings of liberation, we learn to be,
The architects of our own destiny.

Unchaining the Heart

In the depths of the soul, shadows reside,
Memories linger, where love tried to hide.
With each gentle breath, release all the pain,
Unchaining the heart, let peace break the chain.

With hands open wide, let the past drift away,
Embracing the moment, in the soft light of day.
A journey of healing, in every heartbeat,
Where whispers of kindness and courage repeat.

No longer confined by the fear of the night,
Awakening dreams, embracing the light.
Together we stand, letting go of the night,
In the freedom of now, everything feels right.

Each step we take, a path towards the sun,
Unchaining the heart, the journey's begun.
With love as our guide, fears turn to dust,
In the dance of existence, we find our trust.

Rise, oh sweet spirit, let your colors unfurl,
In the garden of hope, let your beauty swirl.
Unchaining the heart from the weight of the past,
In the now we discover, our joy unsurpassed.

The Dawn of Release

As shadows retreat, dawn breaks the sky,
Whispers of morning, a soft lullaby.
In the glow of the new, burdens grow light,
The dawn of release, a beautiful sight.

With every heartbeat, a promise unfolds,
Stories of strength in the silence retold.
Letting go of the night, embracing the glow,
The dawn of release, where possibilities flow.

Each ray a reminder, of hope's sweet embrace,
A tapestry woven, time cannot erase.
In the stillness of dawn, we find our own way,
With courage ignited, we welcome the day.

No more looking back, the past fades away,
In the light of the morn, we no longer sway.
Step into the warmth, let the shadows all cease,
And dance in the dawn of a heart made at peace.

Awake, oh my spirit, to life's tender song,
The dawn of release, where we all belong.
Together in harmony, love lights our flight,
With wings of the morning, let's glow in the light.

Shadows Shed

In the twilight of change, we shed our guise,
Letting go of the past, as the old self dies.
With each tear that falls, we wash ourselves clean,
Shadows shed softly, bringing new sheen.

A river of moments, flowing so free,
Each current a heartbeat, a chance to just be.
The weight of the world, dissolved in the stream,
In the light of the now, we nourish the dream.

Every struggle endured, a lesson in grace,
Breaking through barriers, we find our own place.
In the embrace of the dawn, fears fade away,
As shadows shed gently, ushering day.

With courage as armor, we rise from the ground,
In unity's promise, our voices resound.
Together we journey, together we tread,
In the light of our truth, where shadows are shed.

Celebrate the moment, let laughter ignite,
In the tapestry woven, we find pure delight.
As shadows fall softly, love's essence is fed,
In the beauty of being, where darkness has fled.

Wildflower Awakening

In the dawn's gentle light, so free,
Wildflowers awaken, dancing with glee.
Colors burst forth, a vivid display,
Nature's canvas brightens the day.

Bees hum softly, a sweet melody,
Petals unfold in a dreamy spree.
Sun-kissed blooms sway in cool morning air,
Whispers of spring, a fragrance so rare.

Amidst the green, they sway and twirl,
Each one a story in this vibrant world.
In fields of gold, they paint the scene,
A testament to life's wondrous sheen.

From roots deep in soil, to skies above,
They celebrate existence, a song of love.
In every flower, hope finds its place,
A reminder of beauty, wrapped in grace.

As twilight descends, the colors fade,
Yet still they dream in the evening shade.
Tomorrow they'll bloom, a sight to behold,
In wildflower whispers, life stories told.

The Call of the Untamed

In rugged hills where the wild winds blow,
The call of the untamed begins to grow.
Ancient forests whisper old tales anew,
A symphony played by the brave and the true.

Mountains stand tall, guardians of time,
Inviting the wanderers, lost in their prime.
Rivers run wild, carving paths so free,
A dance with the earth, a primal decree.

Stars shine vividly in the night's embrace,
Each twinkle a guide, a celestial trace.
The moon casts shadows on wilderness wide,
Where secrets unfold, and dreams can't abide.

Creatures roam freely in nature's domain,
Echoing the heartbeat, a soft, steady strain.
Wildflowers bloom where the wild winds play,
Each petal a whisper, a promise to stay.

Let the spirit soar, unchained and alive,
In earth's wild beauty, we truly thrive.
Embrace the call, let adventure ignite,
The untamed awaits in the depth of the night.

Windswept and Wandering

Through valleys low and mountains steep,
Windswept whispers stir from sleep.
The call of adventure, a sweet refrain,
Pulls the wanderer back again.

Paths less traveled, beckon the soul,
In the arms of nature, we become whole.
With each step taken, horizons expand,
The world reveals wonders, unplanned.

Meadows of gold under vast, blue skies,
Where dreams take flight and spirits rise.
Every gust carries tales of the past,
Memories woven, forever to last.

From ocean's roar to the forest's sigh,
Windswept and wandering, we learn to fly.
With hearts wide open, we chase the breeze,
In moments of stillness, we find our peace.

As twilight softens and day turns to night,
The stars above twinkle, a guiding light.
Forever we wander, forever we roam,
In the embrace of the winds, we find our home.

Cascading into Freedom

In mountains high, where the waters gleam,
Cascades rush forth, a powerful dream.
Flowing like whispers, wild and unchained,
A symphony of nature, perfectly ordained.

Rushing and tumbling, over rocks they glide,
Breaking the silence, a joyous ride.
Each drop a story, each spray a laugh,
In the dance of the river, we find our path.

Trees line the banks, guardians so wise,
Watching the beauty as life multiplies.
With every ripple, a new chance to start,
A cascade of freedom, a quenching of heart.

Under the sun's glow, colors collide,
The journey of water, a beautiful tide.
From mountain to valley, it carves its decree,
In the rush of the moment, we feel truly free.

As twilight descends, the flow softly slows,
Yet dreams keep cascading, as nighttime bestows.
In the heart of the wild, our spirits take flight,
Cascading into freedom, a dance of pure light.

Unbound Spirits

In shadows we dance, wild and free,
We chase the moonlight, bold as the sea.
Each heartbeat echoes, strong and loud,
Together we rise, unbroken, unbowed.

A fire ignites in every soul,
Dreams take flight, each spirit whole.
We soar on wings, no tether in sight,
Unbound, we embrace the lingering night.

The past may linger, a distant song,
Yet here we stand, where we belong.
With winds of freedom, we chart our course,
Unbound spirits, a mighty force.

Through storms we'll wander, lush and vast,
With courage in heart, we break from the past.
No chains to hold, just feet on the ground,
In unity's strength, our peace is found.

Let whispers of hope guide our way,
In every dawn, a brand new day.
Together we stand, hand in hand,
Unbound spirits, a vibrant band.

Escape from Conformity

I walk the line, yet feel confined,
A world of rules, so well-defined.
But deep inside, a fire sparks,
A craving for freedom, bright as the marks.

I shed my fears, let shadows fade,
In the mirror's gaze, a choice is made.
To break the mold, to dance my tune,
Beneath the sun, beneath the moon.

With every step, I feel the thrill,
An anthem rising, chasing the chill.
The courage blooms, like flowers in spring,
In the grasp of fate, I learn to sing.

Let voices clash, let silence break,
For every heart, there's a path to make.
In the journey's ache, we find our place,
As rebels born of grace and space.

No longer tethered by someone's design,
In glorious chaos, our spirits align.
The taste of freedom, the pulse of the new,
In the escape, we find what is true.

Together we rise, unyielding, strong,
In a world reborn, we all belong.
No box can hold us, no chains can bind,
In the heart of the brave, true love we find.

The Whisper of Independence

A gentle breeze speaks soft and low,
To all who listen, its wisdom flows.
With every rustle, a message clear,
The whisper of independence draws near.

In solitude's embrace, I hear the call,
A strength that rises, unmarked by fall.
Each choice, a step on the path untamed,
With every heartbeat, my spirit claimed.

The sky above, a vast expanse,
Invites me forward, invites me to dance.
With wings unfurled, I seek the skies,
In the whisper of freedom, my spirit flies.

The chains of doubt begin to break,
As dreams awaken, the past forsake.
In the silent courage, a flame ignites,
Guiding my heart through the darkest nights.

In the echoes of time, my voice stands tall,
With every heartbeat, I heed the call.
For independence is a song divine,
In the whispers of night, my soul will shine.

So let me dance in the wild and free,
Braving the tides, just me being me.
In unity's light, my essence glows,
The whisper of independence forever flows.

Reclaiming the Sky

The clouds above, a canvas gray,
Yet deep within, I long to play.
With colors bright, I'll paint my way,
Reclaiming the sky at break of day.

Each star awaits, a twinkling spark,
To guide the heart from shadows dark.
With hope ablaze, I'll take my flight,
Reclaiming the sky, my soul ignites.

In the depths of night, potential gleams,
A tapestry woven of vibrant dreams.
With courage stitched in every seam,
I rise above, I dare to beam.

No limits here, just endless space,
A heart that knows this sacred place.
With every breath, my spirit flies,
Unfurl the heart, reclaim the skies.

Through storms and winds, I'll never sway,
In strength and grace, I find my way.
The sky's embrace, a warm delight,
Reclaiming my dreams, I take to flight.

So in the dawn, as colors bloom,
I paint my path, dispelling gloom.
With wings of hope, I'll greet the high,
Reclaiming the sky, forever I'll fly.

The Echo of Echoes

In the woods, a whisper flows,
Each branch sways where the silence glows.
Footsteps dance on a misty ground,
Lost voices linger, a haunting sound.

Through valleys deep, the shadows creep,
Legend speaks of secrets to keep.
Nature's call in a twilight's breath,
Whispers fade, but never death.

The calls of night, the moon's embrace,
A tapestry spun in empty space.
Memories echo, faint yet strong,
In every heartbeat, where we belong.

From the past, the stories rise,
Like fireflies under starry skies.
With each echo, a tale reborn,
Woven threads in the fabric worn.

At dawn's light, the echoes dance,
In morning's glow, we take the chance.
To remember all who spoke before,
In the echo of echoes, forevermore.

Grounded No More

Once I stood on solid ground,
But now my heart is unbound.
Winds of change swept through my soul,
In new horizons, I find my goal.

Roots that bound me, now I sever,
In the skies, I drift forever.
Clouds embrace my fleeting dreams,
In a realm where freedom gleams.

Daring steps on paths unknown,
Every whisper feels like home.
Guided by the stars above,
I chase my spark, I chase my love.

With wings outstretched, I soar so high,
No limits now as I touch the sky.
From grounded ties, I set apart,
In every moment, I find my heart.

With every turn, new views I see,
In this journey, I'm truly free.
The world below fades from my sight,
Grounded no more, I reclaim my flight.

The Sun in My Eyes

A golden ray spills on the ground,
In its warmth, a joy is found.
Colors burst, the world awakes,
In this glory, my spirit shakes.

With each dawn, a promise made,
In shadows long, fears start to fade.
The sun ignites what's left inside,
A beacon bright, a fearless guide.

Dreams unfold in the morning light,
Chasing shadows into the night.
The sun in my eyes, I rise and shine,
In its embrace, my heart aligns.

Golden fields and endless skies,
In every heartbeat, the sun replies.
Lighting pathways, banishing strife,
With every heartbeat, I embrace life.

The sun in my eyes, I find my place,
In its glow, I feel the grace.
A dance of warmth, a song of cheer,
With the sun in my eyes, I conquer fear.

When Doubt Breaks Apart

In the stillness, a whisper grows,
Seeds of doubt in the heart, it sows.
Questions linger, shadows cast,
Challenging the echoes of the past.

When uncertainty calls at the night,
It dims the spark, it steals the light.
In murky waters, I start to wade,
Fear holds tight, but hope won't fade.

But as the dawn begins to break,
Cracks of doubt begin to shake.
Each ray of light, a gentle touch,
Dismantling fears, it means so much.

With every step, I gather strength,
Pushing past the shadows' length.
When doubt breaks apart, I stand tall,
Knowing that I can rise through it all.

In the end, it's courage's art,
To mend the pieces and restart.
When doubt subsides and hope ignites,
A brighter path comes into sight.

The Echo of Selves Unlocked

In quiet corners of the mind,
Our echoes dance, untamed, unconfined.
Whispers of dreams that softly glide,
Uncover truths we often hide.

Reflections shimmer in the night,
Flickering, shaping our inner light.
Voices of past and future collide,
A symphony of selves inside.

With every breath, we learn to see,
The boundless nature of what can be.
Through open hearts, we come alive,
In the mirror, our spirits thrive.

A journey mapped by stars above,
Each echo wrapped in endless love.
Together we rise, unmasked, unchained,
In our essence, forever sustained.

In this moment, we embrace our core,
Each echo a part of the evermore.
Unlocking doors to what's unknown,
We find ourselves, and we are home.

The Fire of Determination

In the heart burns a fierce flame,
Fueled by visions, no two the same.
With every stoke, a promise made,
To rise above, not to be swayed.

Through shadows thick and mountains high,
The fire glows, illuminating the sky.
It whispers strength against the night,
A beacon bold, a guiding light.

With every challenge, embers flare,
Igniting passion, and we dare.
To face the fears that hold us back,
In the heart of the storm, we find our track.

Resilience forged in trials sent,
The fire fuels each brave intent.
Together we rise, undaunted, free,
With every heartbeat, we decree.

In the blaze of will, we find our way,
Through darkest night to brightest day.
The fire of determination burns bright,
A testament to our inner fight.

Sailing Beyond Boundaries

With sails unfurled, we catch the wind,
Adventure calls, the world begins.
Horizon stretches, vast and wide,
Where dreams and courage intertwine.

Each wave a lesson, a song to learn,
In tides of change, our spirits burn.
Navigating storms and endless seas,
Guided by stars and whispered pleas.

To shores unknown, we set our course,
Fueled by passion, our inner force.
With every heartbeat, we embrace,
The thrill of freedom in this race.

Boundaries fade as we explore,
New depths await on every shore.
In unity, we find our way,
Sailing beyond limits, come what may.

With every journey, we grow anew,
In the ocean's heart, we find our hue.
Together we weave our endless tale,
In the winds of change, we shall prevail.

From Roots to Wings

Deep in the earth, our roots run wide,
Anchored strong where dreams reside.
From muddy waters, we find our strength,
As time unfolds in endless length.

The branches stretch to meet the sky,
With every leaf, we dare to fly.
From whispered winds on summer nights,
We gather dreams, igniting flights.

Each heartbeat tells a story true,
Of battles won and visions new.
Together we rise, like birds in spring,
Embracing the joy that freedom brings.

With roots that ground and wings that soar,
We find our place, forevermore.
In the dance of life, we intertwine,
From earth to sky, our spirits shine.

In every sunset, there lies a chance,
To leap into the vast expanse.
From roots to wings, we shall embrace,
The beauty found in every space.

The Reckoning of Roots

In the soil where dreams take flight,
Ancestors whisper under moonlight.
Their stories woven deep in the ground,
Echoes of choices, forever profound.

Branches reach high, yet roots run deep,
In the heart of the earth, secrets keep.
A testament to trials faced,
Each scar a memory, wisely placed.

From the shadows, strength does rise,
Nurtured by love, not just goodbyes.
Through storms and trials, we stand tall,
Bound to our past, yet free to call.

The reckoning comes, a time to see,
How far we've come, who we can be.
In the mirror of time, we find our way,
With every heartbeat, in light and gray.

Roots intertwine, a web so wide,
In unity, we find our pride.
For in each reckoning, clear and bright,
There lies the promise of endless light.

In Search of Open Skies

With a heart unbound, I roam the plains,
Chasing the sun, ignoring the chains.
Through valleys and hills, I wander free,
In search of horizons calling to me.

The clouds drift softly, a canvas so vast,
Painting my dreams, both present and past.
I breathe in the winds, tastes of the sea,
Yearning for peace, just to be me.

The mountains beckon, high and bold,
Whispers of secrets, waiting to unfold.
I follow their call, step by step,
In search of the skies where hopes are kept.

A compass of stars guides me each night,
While shadows fade, and new paths ignite.
With every horizon, new stories arise,
In search of freedom under open skies.

Through fields of gold, where dreams collide,
I find my journey, the heart as my guide.
Together we soar, like birds in flight,
Embracing the dawn, chasing the light.

The Unseen Passage

In the silence of twilight, a door ajar,
Leading to realms where the wonders are.
Invisible paths woven in time,
A dance of shadows, a silent chime.

Along hidden corridors where secrets hide,
Echoes of laughter in the flow of the tide.
Glimmers of stories that time forgot,
Searching for meaning in the threads we caught.

Each step we take, an unfolding chase,
Through the fabric of dreams, we find our place.
An unseen passage, a mystical guide,
With every heartbeat, we slip inside.

As the night deepens, illusions fade,
In the heart of silence, memories are made.
We embrace the unknown with courage anew,
For this unseen passage leads me to you.

In the tapestry woven of dusk and dawn,
The unseen passage keeps us drawn.
Echoes of life in the depth of the night,
Guide us together, in love's pure light.

Adrift in Possibility

On waves of thought, I drift and sway,
In oceans of dreams, I find my way.
Each current whispers, urging me near,
Adrift in the vastness, I conquer fear.

The horizon beckons, a shimmer of chance,
Whirling in rhythms, I learn to dance.
With every heartbeat, the world unfolds,
Tales of adventure in whispers retold.

In the arms of the wind, I sail so free,
Discovering realms where my spirit can be.
The stars above twinkle, a guiding light,
Adrift in possibility, I embrace the night.

As worlds collide, I find my spark,
In the canvas of life, I leave my mark.
With hope as my anchor, love as my creed,
Adrift in possibility, I plant each seed.

Together we rise, like tide and foam,
In the dance of destiny, I feel at home.
Floating through moments, a joyous spree,
Adrift in possibility, forever free.